Praise for The Budgetnista

Melissa ▮▮▮ Thanks again Tiffany TheBudgetnista! You SAVED my life literally! to some it's may be just money but everything was at stake for me. God bless you!!!

The Whole Woman Project shared your photo.
The Budgetnista is not just telling you how to get out of debt but she keeps it real about her getting out of debt. Love The Budgetnista.

Allison ▮▮▮ ▶ **Tiffany TheBudgetnista**
1 hr ·

Thanks Tiffany TheBudgetnista you make budgeting and saving so much fun. 😊

Lauren ▮▮▮ Lol! Tiffany TheBudgetnista, you really have no clue how many times a day your name, or the name of your group is mentioned in this household! You have truly changed the way the hubby and I look at money and credit! I thank you and I hope that people don't scroll past this post but instead actually get involved and get right! 😊

Maya ▮▮▮ @Educ8Money2Kids · 12m
Love how @TheBudgetnista defines money. Money is a tool. It can be used to build or destroy your financial life. YOU determine how it's used

Rachel ▮▮▮ @TheBelleAgency · 27 Dec
Was able to lower my car insurance today after going deeper into @TheBudgetnista's book. Y'all are sleeping if you haven't gotten it yet.

Praise for The Budgetnista

Lorraine 23 hours ago `LINKED COMMENT`
Oh my gosh! I think you are wonderful!! Come Jan 1 I'm planning on paying down my debt!! You came along at a PERFECT time! Your plan makes so much sense! Your book is on its way!! You are a God send!! I'll keep in touch to let you know how it's going. While waiting for the book I'll be watching your YouTube videos! I'm so excited!!! Thank you for sharing your knowledge! ~Lorraine

Radiant Yes ! Yes! Tiffany TheBudgetnista is defying all types of gender bias, stereotypes, and shattering glass ceilings in the financial advising profession! She getting all bicostal, cross-gender, and multi-socioeconomic..Go head Tiff!!!

Side note: I sincerely appreciate this awe-inspiring group of individuals. ((((Virtual Hugs))))

Elizabeth
Today I took the first step in living the way I would like instead of waiting for the lottery to bless me I was able to make a sizeable donation to a friend's business, and I couldn't stop talking about how you helped make it possible, Tiffany TheBudgetnista Aliche! One of my goals this year is to support projects that help us grow as a community. Some people think I have a lot of money, but a little bit at a time adds up to something great!

Like · Comment · Stop Notifications · 3 hours ago via mobile

Latrice Tiffany TheBudgetnista, I just finished listening to your podcast interview and it is inspiring to know that someone just like everyone else has experienced financial hardships that are relatable to ours and is not judgemental; but enjoy sharing your wealth of information to help the rest of us to live or best lives. Thanks!

Praise for the Live Richer Challenge

Khalilah ▬▬▬▬▬▬ Keep me posted Tiffany TheBudgetnista if they want someone on the East Coast! The whole challenge was a huge blessing for me! The biggest benefit I received from the challenge is a new mindset. My thinking has totally been transformed as a result of the LRC. That is priceless and something that can never be taken away from me!!! #Blessed and thanks again Tiffany for the passionate work that you do!

1 min · Unlike · 👍 1

Chiniqua ▬▬▬ ▶ **Dream Catchers : LIVE RICHER**
16 hrs ·

I've been in this group for a while and never posted anything. Just wanted to share a little today. Before I started the challenge I had a maxed out credit card, all of my bills were past due, I had multiple pay day loans, and a credit score in the 400s. I had a shopping problem and continued to shop and waste money knowing my bills weren't paid. Sometimes I had to borrow money from my mother to get to work. It took an eviction notice and my cable getting cut off for me to wake up.

I found the challenge and it really helped me to get my priorities straight. It took a lot of hard work. I had to cut everything that was not necessary out of my budget. No shopping trips. No spending $15 a day eating out. No buying expensive gifts. I learned to do my own hair and nails. I bring my lunch everyday. I learned how to coupon and actually enjoy being cheap.

I'm finally caught up on all my bills, credit card is paid off, and I even opened my first savings account. It feels so good knowing I don't owe money to anyone and have a little nest egg. Thanks Tiffany for creating the challenge and everyone in the group for all the great advice you post. 😊

LIVE RICHER CHALLENGE. Copyright © 2014

The Budgetnista and its logo, $B, are trademarks of Tiffany Aliche.

No part of this book may be reproduced or transmitted in any form or by any means, electronic or mechanically, including photocopying, recording, or by any information storage and retrieval system without written permission from the publisher. For more information, contact Tiffany Aliche at tiffany@thebudgetnista.com.

Disclaimer:
This book is designed to provide accurate and reliable information on the subject of personal finance, sold with the understanding that neither the author nor publisher is engaged in representation of legal, accounting or other professional services by publishing this book. As each individual situation is unique, any relevant personal finance questions should be addressed with an appropriate professional. Doing so ensures the situation will be evaluated professionally, carefully and properly. The author and publisher specifically disclaim any liability, loss, or risk incurred as an outcome, directly or indirectly, through the use and application of any contents of this work.

Visit the website:
www.thebudgetnista.com

To the Unicorn Squad:

Thank you for helping me make magic happen every day.

Tiffany

Let's get to know each other.

Hi, I'm Tiffany! Welcome to the *LIVE RICHER Challenge: Homebuying Edition*. If you're thinking about buying a home and wondering what it takes to become a homeowner, we've got you covered.

"Live Richer" means to purposefully and passionately design the life you deserve. The purpose of the *LIVE RICHER Challenge: Homebuying Edition* is to teach you the basics of saving to qualify for the home of your dreams. In our lifetime, a home is one of the biggest purchases we make. This challenge helps you navigate this major purchase with confidence.

I received a sound financial education growing up, which helped me buy my first home at 26. Still, I haven't always made the best money choices. I love to share my story because it proves that no matter how bad a situation may seem, it's possible to dig your way out.

Tiffany's Financial Fiascos

1. At age 24, I took a $20,000 cash advance from my credit card, investing it with a "friend." This genius move landed me in $35,000 worth of debt just a few months later.

2. At age 26, I bought my first home right before the housing bubble burst. The value of my $220,000 condo declined to $150,000 during the Great Recession.

3. At age 30, I lost my job during the recession and was unable to keep up with my bills. The credit score of 802 I once enjoyed quickly plummeted to 574.

When I lost my home, I had to move in with my parents. Pretty bad, huh? Once I adopted my LIVE RICHER lifestyle, I was able to pay off my credit card debt in two and a half years, make peace with my mortgage lender, and raise my credit score almost 200 points over a two-year period.

Within the last few years, I've also been able to travel to over 30 countries. Most recently, I paid for a new home in cash.

Now, I use the solutions that helped me during my "financial fiascos" as a tool to guide people like you who want to do the same.

In 2008, I started The Budgetnista, an award-winning professional and educational services firm. As "The Budgetnista," I'm a spokesperson who speaks, writes, teaches and creates financial education products and services that include seminars, workshops, curricula, and training.

I've written a #1 Amazon bestseller, *The One Week Budget,* which teaches readers how to budget their income and automate the process in just seven days. In 2015, I launched the first edition of another #1 Amazon bestseller, *LIVE RICHER Challenge,* which has helped over 700,000 women across the world save and pay off millions. This book is the **fifth** in my LIVE RICHER series.

You can learn more about me and The Budgetnista at www.thebudgetnista.com.

Why do this challenge?

Have you ever asked yourself any of these questions?

1. How much do I need to save for a home?
2. How much money do I need for a down payment?
3. What mortgage is the best one for me?
4. What credit score do I need to qualify for a mortgage?
5. What's the step-by-step homebuying process?

If so, great! This challenge will answer these questions - plus more! I even promise to do it in a straightforward way that'll be easy for you to implement. In just 22 days, you'll have a plan in place to buy your next home.

HOW TO READ THIS BOOK

Are you ready to learn about homebuying? Good, let's get to work.

How it works:
Each day I'll assign an Easy Financial Task designed to help you get and stay on the road to success.

The daily tasks will focus on the money theme of the week. The weekly themes for the *LIVE RICHER Challenge: Homebuying Edition* are:

Week 1: Homebuying Knowledge
Week 2: Home Loan Requirements
Week 3: The Home Loan Process
Final Day: LIVE RICHER

How to guarantee your success:
- Every morning, read and commit to the Easy Financial Task.

- Perform the task. Don't worry... it won't be hard.

- **Get an accountability partner(s). The best way to rock this challenge is to partner up with at least one other person and work together. It'll keep you motivated. You can also reach out to and work with other Dream Catchers (the name I've given to folks working on the challenge), in the private LIVE RICHER group at www.livericherchallenge.com**

- Go to the www.livericherchallenge.com book resources page to get the Challenge Starter Kit which includes the calendar, worksheets, and other downloadables you'll need to complete this challenge.

- Share your experiences with me, ask questions, and leave comments via social media. Here's where you can find me online:

The Budgetnista Blog: thebudgetnistablog.com
Twitter & Instagram: @TheBudgetnista
Facebook: The Budgetnista

I've also created many awesome resources for you that can't fit into this book. You can find them for *free* at www.livericherchallenge.com.

LIVE RICHER,
Tiffany "The Budgetnista" Aliche

Table of Contents

Week 1: Homebuying Knowledge

Homebuying Knowledge Week Goals 15
Day 1: Homebuying Goals 16
Day 2: Purchasing Methods 20
Day 3: Your Capacity 23
Day 4: Qualifying Income 26
Day 5: Debt-to-Income 28
Day 6: Review, Reflect, Relax 30
Day 7: Weekly Inspiration 31

Week 2: Home Loan Requirements

Home Loan Requirements Week Goals 37
Day 8: Your Character 38
Day 9: Your Capital 42
Day 10: Popular Home Loans 46
Day 11: Ways to Save 52
Day 12: Special Housing Programs 55
Day 13: Review, Reflect, Relax 59
Day 14: Weekly Inspiration 60

Week 3: The Home Loan Process

The Home Loan Process Week Goals 63
Day 15: Your Collateral 64
Day 16: Mortgage Insurance 66
Day 17: Compliance 17
Day 18: Your Home Team 72
Day 19: The Loan Process 75
Day 20: Review, Reflect, Relax 78
Day 21: Weekly Inspiration 79

Table of Contents

LIVE RICHER

Live Richer goal: Celebrate completing the challenge and complete the "Dream Home" activity.

Day 22: LIVE RICHER 81

WEEK 1: HOMEBUYING KNOWLEDGE

THIS WEEK'S GOAL:

Learn homebuying basics, including the methods of purchasing a home. If you choose a mortgage, learn how lenders review income to determine how much you can afford.

Live Richer Challenge: Homebuying Edition
Day 1: Homebuying Goals

Week 1: Homebuying Knowledge

Today's Easy Financial Task: Identify, write down, and share your homebuying goals.

How to rock this task:
- List your homebuying goals.
- Get acquainted with the format of this challenge.

Welcome to the first week of the LRC: Homebuying Edition! Woot! Woot!

This first week sets up the basics you need to know about buying a home. This is one of the biggest purchases many of us make in our lifetime, and navigating the process of making such a large purchase can make you a bit anxious. Not to worry, though!

I'm here to break down the basics of buying a home in simple steps to help you prepare for your next purchase. Whether you want to buy within the next few months or the next few years, the LRC: Homebuying Edition will offer some guidance to help you fulfill your dreams of becoming a homeowner.

Partnering with me throughout this challenge is Netiva "The Frugal Creditnista" Heard, who is a credit expert and realtor.

Before starting this challenge, we want to cover the very basics, starting with one important question...

Are you ready to buy a home?
Here are some ways to know if you're ready to buy:

1) You plan on staying in one location for a while. Unless you're buying an investment property, be reasonably sure you're ready to lay down roots in a specific location before buying a home there.

2) There is no big-ticket item or experience you'd like first. Once you get a house, that dream trip, hot car, new business venture, etc., may have to wait. The money you once had in excess will probably be reduced during the first few years as a new homeowner. Is this a sacrifice you're willing to make?

3) You've consulted your *future* MONTHLY budget. This is the budget you'll be living on once you own a home. After doing said budget, ask yourself - after all of your expenses are taken care of...AND I MEAN ALL TAKEN CARE OF (old bills, utilities, new home expenses, entertainment, groceries, etc.), will you still have money left over to save? You should. Do the math. If your current income won't cover your future expenses *and* leave you with money left over to save, you can't afford to buy a home.

4) You're currently saving your new (home) expenses each month. If you *really* want to know if you're financially ready to buy a home, begin paying your mortgage and new home expenses to yourself in a savings account now (minus your rent). If you can't pay a mortgage now, then you won't be able to "magically" pay your mortgage later.

5) You LOVE or at least like your job. If you own a home and hate your job, it will be very difficult to leave a steady paycheck (despite the soul-crushing stress), because of your financial obligations (mortgage). If you don't love what you're doing and are renting, you can always leave for something else that may pay less, because moving to a cheaper place is a solution. Although a hassle, moving is much easier when you're renting.

6) You're looking for a mortgage on a home that is rentable. That means if times get financially rough and you have to move to a cheaper apartment, parent's house, or friend's couch, could you rent your home and COMPLETELY cover your mortgage, taxes, and insurance? Figure this out by comparing the rent of similar homes in the area where you are considering buying. Structure your deal to make your mortgage the same or under what those homes rent for. This might involve putting down a large down payment, reducing how much you pay for a home or paying for discount points to reduce the interest rate. (We'll cover how to save for a down payment and what discount points are later in this challenge.)

7) Make sure it's something YOU really want. I bought a home because I thought it was what I was "supposed" to do as a responsible adult (25 at the time). Not so. There's nothing wrong with renting. Renting is NOT throwing your money away, but allows more financial freedom. Renting for a while is what made it possible for me to start a business and travel the world. Buying for the **RIGHT** reasons is good too, though.

The First Two Tasks
Now that we've covered some things to think about before buying, let's head right into the first few tasks of this challenge.

First, write down two goals that you have for the LRC: Homebuying Edition. Here are a few good examples:

1. By the end of this challenge, I want to learn strategies to save for my down payment.
2. By the end of this challenge, I want to learn down payment programs I can qualify for to buy a house.
3. By the end of this challenge, I want to know what credit score I need to qualify for different home loan products.

Don't miss this step! Write your goals down on the next page. Setting tangible goals for this challenge is important because:

1. Identifying and writing down goals gives you a mission to fulfill as you're completing tasks.
2. Writing down goals gives them power.
3. Writing down goals holds you accountable.

Your final task for today is to pick an accountability partner(s).

Choose a friend or get with a group of people who are taking the challenge with you so you can keep each other on track.

You can also head into the Dream Catcher Facebook Group to find other Dream Catchers who are working through the challenge. Join the Facebook Group at www.livericherchallenge.com.

Homebuying Edition Goal Sheet by The Budgetnista

For the first task of the LRC: Homebuying Edition, I want you to write down two goals that you have for the Challenge.

Don't miss this step! Setting tangible goals is important because:
- Identifying and writing down your goals gives you a mission to fulfill as you're completing tasks.
- Writing down goals gives them power.
- Sharing your goals holds you accountable.

Here are a few examples of good goals:
- By the end of this Challenge, I want to learn strategies to save for my down payment.
- By the end of this Challenge, I want to learn down payment programs I can qualify for to buy a house.
- By the end of this Challenge, I want to know what credit score I need to qualify for different loan products.

Be sure to make your goals actionable.

Goal #1 _____
_____
_____
_____

Goal #2 _____
_____
_____
_____

Live Richer Challenge: Homebuying Edition
Day 2: Purchasing Methods

Today's Easy Financial Task: Learn home purchasing methods.

How to rock this task:
- Learn the various ways to purchase a home.
- Learn the 5 C's of Credit used by lenders to qualify you for a home.
- Choose the method(s) you are considering for your home purchase.

Welcome to the second day of the challenge!

Yesterday you wrote down a few goals. Now, we're ready to dig into some of the basics of homebuying. Woot! Woot!

Methods of Buying a Home
There are several ways you can purchase a home besides the traditional mortgage. Before we get into the nitty-gritty of mortgages, let's discuss the alternatives.

Cash - Yes, some people do purchase houses in cash. In fact, I purchased my home last year in cash. What's so great about cash? If you have the cash on hand, a cash offer can help you win a bidding war in a hot market, and you don't have to worry about a monthly payment.

A drawback of buying with cash is that you aren't able to use that money for other reasons. For instance, you could invest that money instead of using it for a home purchase. If you have a stockpile of cash, you should speak with a financial advisor first to see if it's a smart choice.

Seller financing/land contract - Seller financing and a land contract is a unique type of financing where the seller lends money to the borrower. You set up a payment agreement that includes interest and the terms. Often, these types of financing are short-term and have a balloon payment at the end.

The seller financing or land contract may be worthwhile if you're having trouble qualifying for a mortgage from a lender. It can also be faster than going through the entire application process with a lender who checks your credit and does the whole underwriting thing.

A drawback of borrowing from the seller: the interest rate may be high. A short-term loan with a balloon payment can be difficult to manage. Balloon payments may be several times your monthly payment or the entire balance of your loan.

Rent to own or Rent with option - This type of purchasing method works exactly like the name. You enter an agreement with the seller to "rent to buy" or "rent with the option of buying." A portion of the rent you're paying before buying may be applied to your down payment. At the end of the agreement, you make the purchase. Depending on the agreement, you may have an option to change your mind.

Mortgage financing - We've arrived at the most popular method of purchasing a home — **the mortgage!** A mortgage is a home loan where a lender or bank lends you money to buy. You make a down payment, which is typically given to the seller in cash. The seller gets the rest of the money from the mortgage and you pay the mortgage back to the lender, with interest.
In order to obtain a loan, lenders do a review of your income, employment and credit to decide if they want to lend to you.

Lenders use the 5 C's of Credit to decide whether they want to lend you the money you need for a house.

For the rest of this challenge, we'll be reviewing the 5 C's in detail, but here's a brief overview:

The 5 C's of Credit — Factors Lenders Review to Approve You

Character - Character is your trustworthiness. Lenders want to lend money to people who are responsible and will pay their money back. Your character and credit play a major role in purchasing a home.

Capacity and Cash Flow - Capacity is your financial ability to pay the loan back. Lenders are checking on your income and employment.

Capital - Capital is the moolah. Do you have money to put down for a house? If you do, how much money will you have left after the purchase? Lenders want to make sure you have some assets to spare even after the purchase.

Conditions - Conditions in the 5 C's stands for market conditions, including interest rates and other factors going on in the housing market that could impact your lender's decision.

Collateral - Collateral is an asset that backs a loan. In this case, your home backs the loan. If you default, the bank or lender can take it. Lenders want to know the value before lending money to ensure they're making a good investment, so an appraisal is done to determine the home's worth.

On to Your Task
Today's task: Write down the purchasing methods you're considering. Financing with a mortgage is undoubtedly the most popular method of buying a home. If you're considering other options, write them down too! Once you're done with that task, you're done for the day!

Any questions? Remember to reach out to your partners to encourage each other throughout the challenge. Check into the Dream Catchers: LIVE RICHER group as well.

What purchasing methods do I plan to use?

_____

_____

_____

_____

_____

Live Richer Challenge: Homebuying Edition
Day 3: Your Capacity

Today's Easy Financial Task: Answer questions about your capacity to borrow.

How to rock this task:
- Learn more about the capacity element of the 5 C's of Credit.
- Answer questions about your capacity to borrow.

We're on to Day 3 of the LRC: Homebuying Edition.

Have you been keeping up with the tasks thus far? If you missed a task, no worries. We have two days at the end of the week for review.

Now — let's talk about capacity!

Borrowing Capacity
Capacity measures your ability to afford a mortgage. More specifically, capacity is if you have enough income and stability to pay off your mortgage in the allotted time, or sooner. Lenders consider:

- Stable employment or income.
- Income to cover the mortgage.
- Income to cover your mortgage plus other debts.
- Income to cover home maintenance and other costs of homeownership.

When you have a consistent job, make a stable income, and work in a stable field, you are showing lenders that you can afford the mortgage now and in the future.

Lenders may question gaps in employment, career changes or layoffs while determining your capacity to repay the loan. Having instability, changes in employment or fluctuations in income could show that you may not be able to manage the loan payment.

Documents to Verify Employment and Income
Lenders will request documents from you to review your employment history. **Generally, two years is the magic number.** Lenders look at the past two to three years as a reflection of what will likely occur in your professional future.

Full-time income that you get a W-2 for at the end of the year makes your life easy. Part-time income, commissions, and income from self-employment can be considered as well, but the income has to be consistent. Lenders may scrutinize this a bit more than income from a typical 9 to 5. You may be asked to provide tax returns, pay stubs or bank statements to prove your income.

If you've been at your job for less than six months, in most cases you will need to submit 30 days of paystubs. If you went through an extended period of unemployment, you need to have been at your current job for at least six months to qualify for a mortgage.

Income from disability and social security income qualify, as well as alimony and child support, as long as you'll be getting that income for two to three years.

Your Task
Today's task is to ask yourself the following preliminary questions:

- Do I have stable employment or income?
- Do I have enough income to comfortably cover a mortgage payment while making other debt payments (i.e. student loans, auto loans, etc.)?
- Do I have enough income to cover home maintenance and other costs of homeownership?

An area to look at to help you answer these questions is your current household cash flow. Do you have money in emergency savings? Do you have money to spare throughout the month?

If so, you may be ready for a house!

If not, you may want to consider taking a look at your budget. Throughout this challenge, we'll be teaching you how much home you can afford, along with saving and budgeting strategies to help you prepare for and manage a home payment.

When you're finished answering the questions, you're done with today's task!

If you want to share your answers, head to the Dream Catchers: Live Richer group. Don't forget to reach out to your accountability partners.

Answer the following questions...

- Do I have stable employment or income?

_____
_____
_____

- Do I have enough income to comfortably cover a mortgage payment while making other debt payments (i.e. student loans, auto loans, etc.)?

_____
_____
_____

- Do I have enough income to cover home maintenance and other costs of homeownership?

_____
_____
_____

Live Richer Challenge: Homebuying Edition
Day 4: Qualifying Income

Today's Easy Financial Task: Determine your qualifying income.

How to rock this task:
- Use the worksheet to write down your qualifying income per month.

Welcome to Day 4 of the LRC: Homebuying Edition!

Yesterday, we discussed the documents that lenders review to qualify you for a mortgage. Today, we're going to take that a step further.

In this task, you will write down each of the types of qualifying income that you have on the Qualifying Income & DTI worksheet. There's a copy at the end of this week.

Make sure you're writing down how much qualifying income you have **per month.** The types of qualifying income include:

- Income from your full-time job
- Income from commissions *
- Income from your part-time job *
- Income from your own business *
- Income from alimony or child support
- Income from disability or social security

* Remember, this income — commissions, part-time jobs, businesses or side hustles — qualifies if you've been steadily earning it over the last two to three years. If not, the lender may not count the income because it's not seen as stable.

Any income you have that isn't stable should be written down on your **inconsistent income column**. This income may become consistent in the next few years. Then, you can bump it over to your qualifying income column.

We're Talkin' Gross

When listing your income, include the **gross income** on this worksheet.

Your gross income is the money you earn before anything is taken out, i.e. taxes. We need the gross income for our task tomorrow, so make sure you write this down!

I also have a VERY special treat for you!

Netiva "The Frugal Creditnista" has an awesome freebie with more information to help you identify the qualifying income you earn.

Go to the livericherchallenge.com book resources Day 4 to access to this freebie.

Don't worry about the debt-to-income (DTI) portion of the Qualifying Income & DTI worksheet. We'll be completing that part tomorrow!

Live Richer Challenge: Homebuying Edition
Day 5: Debt-to-Income

Today's Easy Financial Task: Learn how to calculate your debt-to-income ratio.

How to rock this task:
- Watch the video on DTI.
- Take out your Qualifying Income & DTI worksheet from yesterday.
- Learn what your DTI is.
- Calculate your DTI.

Woot woot! Day 5, and the final day of the first week!

Today we're going to be using the worksheet you filled out yesterday in the back of this week's tasks. This task considers how debt comes into the picture. Besides your income, lenders look at your debt to see if you can manage a mortgage payment. Lenders use a special equation called the debt-to-income ratio, or DTI.

The first task of the day is to watch the video. Check out www.livericher-challenge.com, Day 5 on the book resources tab. When you're done, come back to this page to complete the rest.

What's the DTI?
DTI is a ratio that compares the income you bring in each month to the monthly debts you pay. Here's the equation to calculate your DTI:

Monthly debt payments / Income (the qualifying income you wrote down yesterday) = DTI

Examples of monthly debt responsibilities include:
- Auto loan payments
- Student loan payments
- Personal loan payments
- Child support or alimony payments
- Minimum credit card payments
- Existing mortgage payments

Write Down Your Monthly Debts
After watching the video, pull out your Qualifying Income & DTI worksheet from yesterday.

There's a space for your monthly debts. Write them out. You may need to pull out your bills to be as accurate as possible. Once you've finished listing your monthly debt payments, you can move on to the next step.

Calculate Your DTI
The next step is to calculate your DTI using the monthly income and debt payments on your worksheet. If you haven't done the Qualifying Income & DTI worksheet yet, remember you can find a copy to fill out at the end of this week. Make sure you revisit Day 4's task to complete the qualifying income portion. There are specific types of income that you should be writing down in this column.

What's your DTI?
If you feel comfortable, share your DTI with your accountability partner(s).

Different mortgage products have different requirements of what your DTI can be to qualify. **As a rule of thumb, your DTI should be less than 43 percent.** Again, this limit can vary per product, and lenders may require a different DTI before approving you for a mortgage.

We've reached the end of Day 5 and the end of the tasks for this week!

Tomorrow, you'll review the tasks from the last five days.

Live Richer Challenge: Homebuying Edition
Day 6: Review, Reflect, Relax

Today's Easy Financial Task: Review, Reflect, Relax

How to rock this task:
- *Review* this week's tasks.
- *Reflect* on the LRC: Homebuying Edition tasks.
- *Relax.* Tomorrow we have our final weekly recap video.

Hey hey, we've made it to the end of the first week of the Live Richer Challenge! Take this day to review, reflect, and relax. Today is also a great day to check in on your accountability partner(s). Do they need help with a task?

Do they need some encouragement? Do you both need to catch up on past tasks? Go back through this week.

Live Richer Challenge: Homebuying Edition
Day 7: Weekly Inspiration

Today's Easy Financial Task: Watch the Week 1 Dream Catcher Hangout chat.

How to rock this task:
- Watch the video.
- Listen to words of encouragement.
- Complete challenge tasks you missed.

Today's our first Dream Catcher hangout chat of the LRC: Homebuying Edition!

During the video, we'll discuss the tasks we've worked on this week. We'll also talk about the key takeaways, and you'll hear how other Dream Catchers are working through the challenge.

Make sure to check in on your accountability partner. Have they completed the first week of the challenge? Are they ready for next week?

FYI: Today is a good day to catch up on any tasks that you missed throughout the week. (Make *sure* you've completed the Qualifying Income & DTI worksheet because you'll need it for future challenge days.)

Watch the Dream Catcher hangout at www.livericherchallenge.com under the book resources tab, Day 7: Weekly Inspiration.

Qualifying Income

Write down the qualifying income you earn per month.
Qualifying income may include income you earn from your full-time job, income from commissions, income from your part-time job, income from your own business, income from alimony or child support, and income from disability or social security. You should be writing down pre-tax income; this is gross income before tax or other deductions come out of your paycheck.

Remember: Qualifying income is generally income you've made consistently over the last two to three years. If you have some inconsistent income, such as inconsistent commissions or bonuses, this may not be counted as qualifying income. Put that income in the inconsistent income table to the right for now. If this income becomes stable, you may be able to switch it over to the left column.

Qualifying Income Source	Amount	Inconsistent Income Source	Amount
Ex. Full-time job	$2,500	Ex. Babysitting	$500
	$		$
	$		$
	$		$
	$		$
	$		$
	$		$
	$		$
	$		$
	$		$
	$		$
Total	$	Total	$

DTI worksheet

Write down your monthly debts

In the table below, write down the debt payments you make monthly. Include the minimum payment if you have a credit card bill each month.

Name of Debt	Amount of Monthly Payment
	$
	$
	$
	$
	$
	$
	$
	$
	$
	$
	$
Total	$

Calculate your debt-to-income (DTI) ratio

Use the section below to calculate your debt-to-income ratio. You need to divide your monthly debt payments by your qualifying income and then multiply the result by 100.

_____ ÷ _____ = _____ x 100 = _____%

Monthly Debt Payments   Monthly Qualifying Income   DTI

The Home Loan Process Recap Checklist
Week 1

This Week's Goal: To learn homebuying basics, including the various methods of purchasing a home. If you choose a mortgage, how lenders review income to determine how much you can afford.

- **Day 1:** Homebuying Goals
  - ○ **Easy Financial Task:** Identify, write down, and share your homebuying goals.

- **Day 2:** Purchasing Methods
  - ○ **Easy Financial Task:** Learn home purchasing methods.

- **Day 3:** Your Capacity
  - ○ **Easy Financial Task:** Answer questions about your capacity to borrow.

- **Day 4:** Qualifying Income
  - ○ **Easy Financial Task:** Determine your qualifying income.

- **Day 5:** Debt-to-Income
  - ○ **Easy Financial Task:** Learn how to calculate your debt-to-income ratio.

- **Day 6:** Review, Reflect, Relax
  - ○ **Easy Financial Task:** Review, Reflect, Relax.

- **Day 7:** Weekly Inspiration
  - ○ **Easy Financial Task:** Watch the Week 1 Dream Catcher Hangout chat.

Week 1 Reflections

WEEK 2: HOME LOAN REQUIREMENTS

THIS WEEK'S GOAL:

Understand how credit plays a role in the homebuying process and learn the eligibility requirements for popular homebuying programs.

Live Richer Challenge: Homebuying Edition
Day 8: Your Character

Week 2: Home Loan Requirements

Today's Easy Financial Task: Get your credit reports and scores.

How to rock this task:
- Learn how credit plays a role in the homebuying process.
- Watch a FREE web class on **how I improved my credit score from 547 to 752 in just two years!**
- Check your credit report and score for free.

Welcome to the second week of the LRC: Homebuying Edition!

Did you enjoy the last week's tasks? This week we have an entire new set of tasks that will get you one step closer to buying a home. Let's go!

What's *character* got to do with it?

Last week, I gave you an overview of the 5 C's. They are — character, capacity, capital, conditions, and collateral.

Today we're going to dig into the character element of the 5 C's of Credit.

Character is defined as your trustworthiness and creditworthiness.

Lenders want to lend to borrowers who they determine are responsible and will pay the money back. Your character, or credibility, plays a major role in how they determine whether or not you're qualified.

How does a lender review your character (aka your creditworthiness)? They take a look at your credit reports and credit scores.

When looking at your credit report, lenders usually check:

1. **How much debt you owe:** We talked last week about your debt-to-income ratio and how it tells you and your lender how much home you can afford. (Go back to Day 5 if you missed it.) Lenders look at debt from your credit reports and what you write on your loan application to make this calculation.

2. **Your credit utilization:** Credit utilization is a comparison of your credit balances to your credit limits. To calculate your utilization, divide your credit balances by your credit limits. For example, say you have a:
   a. $1,000 balance on Credit Card A with a limit of $2,000.
   b. $3,000 balance on Credit Card B with a limit of $5,000.
   c. You add up your balances, which equal $4,000.
   d. Then you add up your limits, which equal $7,000.
   e. Divide your balance by the limit ($4,000 / $7,000 = 57%). The ideal credit utilization is below 30%. If you're using a high percentage of your balance, lenders could think you're using it as a crutch, which could make you seem like a less creditworthy candidate.

3. **How long you've had credit history:** Length of credit history is another indicator of your character and creditworthiness. You may be able to qualify for a mortgage with a short credit history, but a long one could also tip the scale in your favor. A long history of managing credit responsibly is an indicator that you'll be a responsible borrower.

4. **If your payments are made on time:** Lenders are looking for evidence of on-time payments. Accounts with positive payment history are a sign to lenders that you're also likely to make on-time mortgage payments.

5. **Any other negative records.** Records like bankruptcy, foreclosures or tax liens will be closely examined on your report. These types of records can be red flags for lenders, but doesn't mean you won't be eligible for a home loan. A certain amount of time has to pass before you can qualify for a home loan after bankruptcy or foreclosures. For example, the waiting period for bankruptcy is two to four years depending on the mortgage. Be honest on your mortgage application about your history. Items may drop off your credit report, but there are other backup systems where your history may show up for lenders.

Your Credit Score

Your credit score is a risk score assigned to you based on the items in your credit history. Lenders also look at your credit score to measure creditworthiness. There are different scoring models used to calculate credit scores.

The one most commonly used by lenders is the FICO score.

Here's how the FICO model calculates your credit score:

• **35% of your score** — *Payment history* — The most important factor is your record of on-time payment history. Late payments will have a major impact on your score. However, a recent history of on-time payments can help improve your score.

• **30% of your score** — *Amounts owed* — How much of the available credit that you're using. The lower the better here, as your credit utilization is considered. Ideally, you want this percentage to be below 30%.

• **15% of your score** — *Length of credit history* — How long you've had different accounts. The older your accounts, the better.

• **10% of your score** — *New credit* — How many hard inquiries you have on your report. Inquiries are credit checks. A lot of credit checks can be a signal that you're overusing debt vehicles. Try to keep your inquiries to a minimum, unless you're shopping around for loan products like mortgages or auto loans. When shopping for these products, multiple inquiries within a 45-day shopping period generally counts as one inquiry.

• **10% of your score** — *Credit mix* — The mix of accounts that you have. Showing that you can manage a mix of credit accounts (aka credit cards) and installment loans (auto loans, a mortgage, etc.) can be good for your score.

Your Tasks for Today

You have four tasks to complete today:

1. **Watch the web class:** Did you know I increased my credit score from 547 to 752 in only TWO YEARS? Take a moment to watch the free workshop on how I made it happen on the www.livericherchallenge.com book resources page, Day 8.

2. **Check your credit report:** To clean up your credit report, you have to know where you stand. There are three credit reporting agencies — Experian, TransUnion, and Equifax. These credit bureaus store your information from creditors. Each year, you're able to get one for free at www.annualcreditreport.com. If you've already used your free credit reports for the year, head down to task number two. I have a solution!

3. **Check your credit scores:** Free credit reports don't come with a credit score, that's why I recommend my favorite place for credit reports and scores...Credit Sesame! Credit Sesame offers free credit scores AND reports. Sign up for free at the www.liverchallenge.com book resources page, Day 8.

4. **Do you need help getting your credit reports in order?** Obtaining and maintaining good credit is key to qualifying for a decent mortgage. Each section of your credit report is important and can have an impact on your score. **Netiva "The Frugal Creditnista" Heard has a 5 Day Credit Challenge that will teach you how to read and break down each section of your credit report.** Grab your access to the free challenge in the book resources page, Day 8.

That's it for today's tasks! Make sure to check in with your accountability partner(s).

Live Richer Challenge: Homebuying Edition
Day 9: Your Capital

Today's Easy Financial Task: Determine how much money you have for a home purchase.

How to rock this task:
- Read the definition of capital.
- Learn the difference between closing costs, down payments, and cash reserves.
- Figure out how much capital you have available for a home.
- Use the SmartAsset Mortgage Calculator to get an idea of how much money you need.

Welcome to the 9th day of the LRC: Homebuying Edition!

Today we're talkin' about capital — dollars, dineros, the big bucks.

The capital element of the 5 C's stands for the liquid assets you use for your home purchase. Liquid assets are assets you can quickly turn into cash and include physical cash, money in deposit accounts, stocks, bonds and CDs. On the other hand, jewelry or property are examples of non-liquid assets.

The capital you have is used for your down payment, closing costs, and cash reserves. Let's discuss what these three things are:

Down Payment

Your down payment is the upfront money you give for the real estate transaction. The down payment required for a mortgage depends on the loan. A down payment generally ranges from 3% to 20%. We'll talk about various loan programs in tomorrow's task!

Closing Costs

Closing costs are necessary to complete a real estate transaction. Closing costs typically cost anywhere from 2% to 6% of the home purchase price. There are several different expenses that are under the "closing costs" umbrella. Some of them are situational. Here's an overview of the most common expenses:

- **Lender origination fees:** Fees lenders charge to process your loan.
- **Discount points:** An extra cost you may pay upfront to lower your interest rate.
- **Title search and title insurance fees:** Before buying a home, a title search is done to make sure no one else has a claim on the property. Title insurance is coverage for you and the lender in case someone should pop up in the future and say they own your new home.
- **Credit report fees:** Lenders charge you for the credit report they pull.
- **Appraisal fees:** An appraisal is done to determine the value of the home tomake sure the lender is lending an appropriate amount. We'll talk more about appraisals next week..
- **Inspection fees:** Home inspections are an important process that you don't want to penny pinch on. Inspections are what alert you to problems with the home before you buy it. I learned this the hard way when a house that I was going to buy was FULL of problems. I recommend getting your inspection FIRST, then the appraisal. If the inspection shows something is seriously wrong with the house, you don't want to pay the extra money for an appraisal.
- **Transfer taxes:** Some states charge transfer and recordation taxes when you transfer ownership of a property from one person to another.
- **Upfront mortgage insurance:** If you pay less than 20% down on a home, there's typically some sort of mortgage insurance that may be charged upfront, and then on a monthly basis to cover the lender in case you default. (We'll discuss this more later.)
- **Homeowners insurance:** Homeowners insurance is protection for your home. Generally, lenders want to see you have insurance at closing.
- **Attorney fees:** In some states, an attorney is required. In others, they are not. If you use an attorney, they will represent you in the transaction.

These fees can add up, but there's a bit of good news. For some mortgages, your seller is allowed to contribute to your closing costs, which is called a **seller concession** or **seller's assist**.

Seller concessions (or seller's assist) can be negotiated into your deal to relieve you of having to pay all of these costs out of pocket.

Cash Reserves

Cash reserves is additional cash you have beyond what's needed for the down payment and closing costs. This is usually several months worth of mortgage payments that you have saved to show lenders you'll be able to handle the mortgage if you run into financial trouble. The cash reserves you need will depend on your situation. Having good credit and a low debt-to-income ratio can help you here. For example, borrowers with a score of 640+ and debt-to-income below 50% typically don't need cash reserves.

Why is having capital important?

The more money you have, the better. Yes — there are mortgage programs that may require little money down upfront, but putting more money down has its benefits. Here are a few:

1. **It can reduce your interest rate.** A low interest rate can save you money over the course of your loan.

2. **A higher down payment can also decrease your monthly payments.** Putting more money down upfront means you owe less money on a loan. This reduces your monthly payment.

3. **It can eliminate mortgage insurance.** We'll cover what mortgage insurance is in detail next week. For an overview, mortgage insurance is an extra cost you pay if you put less than 20% down on a home.

Your Task

Today's task is to run your numbers. Figure out how much capital you have for a down payment, closing costs, and cash reserves.

The SmartAsset Mortgage Calculator (on www.livericherchallenge.com book resources page, Day 9) is an AWESOME tool you can use to find out how much home you can afford, given the capital you have. The calculator breaks down estimated costs and how much capital you may need.

DON'T GET DISCOURAGED: The money you need may seem high at first, but there are mortgage products that require less money down. There are also various programs that we'll cover that may be able to help you cover additional costs.

After reviewing what cash you have and what cash you may need, get excited for tomorrow's task! Tomorrow we're going to run through the details of some popular mortgage products.

Write down the mortgage amount, mortgage payment, downpayment, and any other information you find from the SmartAsset calculator...

_____

_____

_____

_____

_____

_____

_____

_____

Live Richer Challenge: Homebuying Edition
Day 10: Popular Home Loans

Today's Easy Financial Task: Learn about various home loan products.

How to rock this task:
- Read through the guidelines of four popular home loan types.
- Pull out your Qualifying Income & DTI worksheet from last week.
- Compare the DTI you have to these loan guidelines.

Day 10 and we're on to a new task!

Today, we'll be discussing a few popular mortgage programs. There is a decent amount of information in this task, so carve out some time to *carefully* read and understand the mortgage options.

Before we get started, one public service announcement!

Requirements for mortgages can vary from lender to lender. *This overview is just to give you a guideline.* Some programs have minimum requirements, but lenders can choose to be stringent on what they will and won't accept. The good news is, you can shop around with multiple lenders. If you don't meet requirements for one lender, you may meet requirements for another!

Below we discuss: FHA loans, VA loans, USDA loans, and conventional loans. Let's get started!

FHA Loan

Background: The FHA loan is popular because it allows a very low loan payment and perfect credit isn't necessary. This is a government-backed loan that's insured by the Federal Housing Administration (FHA). You do not get this loan directly from the FHA - lenders give you this loan and the FHA insures it. The FHA loan can be used on multi-unit homes (up to four units) as long as the property is your primary residence. There's also the FHA Section 203(K) version of this loan for single-family property rehabs. Looking at a fixer-upper? The FHA loan could be right for you.

Eligibility requirements:

- **Down payment:** 3.5% to 10% depending on your credit score
- **Credit score minimum:** 580+ may qualify you for 3.5% down; 580 or below may qualify you for 10% down
- **Debt-to-income ratio (DTI) maximum:** 50% or lower

Other FHA loan details:

- **Seller contributions:** FHA loans allow the home seller to contribute up to 6% of the home sale price to be applied towards your:
  - Loan origination fees
  - Discount points
  - Credit reporting fees
  - Title charges
  - Homeowners insurance
  - Attorneys fees
  - Inspection fees
  - Any other third party charges that you may incur in the homebuying process

- **Wait periods after adverse credit history:**
  - **Discharged Chapter 7 bankruptcy:** Two-year wait.
  - **Chapter 13 bankruptcy:** Debt doesn't have to be discharged. You can be one year into your payment plan. With timely payments, you can purchase with the trustee's and lenders approval.
  - **Foreclosure, deed in lieu of foreclosure, and short sale:** Three years from the date your name was removed from the title

VA Loan

Background: The VA loan is backed by the U.S. Department of Veteran Affairs for active duty military, select reserve and national guard servicemembers, and certain spouses. The VA loan can also be used on multi-family homes (up to four units) as long as it's your primary residence.

Eligibility requirements:

- **Down payment:** 0%, 5%, or 10% down
- **Credit score:** No credit minimum, but 620 or above is preferred
- **Debt-to-income ratio (DTI):** Maximum is generally 43%

Other VA loan details:

- **Seller contributions:** The VA allows for the seller to contribute 4% of the sales price. The VA is specific on how you can use these contributions.
  - **Here's a list directly from the VA Loan Guide on what seller concessions can include:**
  - Payment of the buyer's VA Funding Fee
  - Prepayment of the buyer's property taxes and insurance
  - Gifts such as a television set or microwave oven
  - Payment of extra points to lower your interest rate
  - Payoff of credit balances or judgments on behalf of the buyer
  - **Seller concessions can not include:**
  - Payment of the buyer's closing costs, or
  - Payment of points as appropriate to the market

- **Wait period after adverse credit history:**
  - **Discharged Chapter 7 bankruptcy:** Two years from the discharge date; no late payments are allowed during this two-year period.
  - **Discharged Chapter 13 bankruptcy:** 12 months of on-time Chapter 13 payments, as long as the trustee approves the new mortgage loan.
  - **Foreclosure, deed in lieu of foreclosure, and short sale:** Three-year wait.
  - **Loan Modification:** One year wait after a loan modification (contingencies apply). *A loan modification is when you change loan terms like interest rate or loan term length to make payments more affordable. Lenders can do this if you're having trouble making payments.*

USDA loan

Background: The USDA loan is another government-backed loan obtained through the U.S. Department of Agriculture. The purpose of this loan is to spur development and encourage homeownership in suburban and rural areas. The USDA loan is only available in specified locations, but you may be surprised to find out that there may be some qualifying places near you. There are income limits for this home loan. Learn more at www.rd.USDA.gov.

Eligibility requirements:

- **Down payment:** 0%
- **Credit score:** 640 typical score; 650 or above is preferred
- **Debt-to-income ratio (DTI):** The maximum is generally 41%

Other USDA details:

- **Seller contributions:** No limit per USDA guidelines; most lenders limit it to 6%. Closing costs can be financed into your loan.

- **Wait period after adverse credit history:**
    - **Discharged Chapter 7 & Chapter 13 bankruptcy:** Three years from discharge date.
    - **Foreclosure:** Three years.
    - **Deed in lieu of foreclosure & short sale:** If you had a number of issues (determined by the lender/USDA), the deed in lieu of foreclosure will be viewed as a foreclosure and you have to wait three years. If your scores are over 640, your underwriter decides if you're eligible to purchase using USDA within one year.

Conventional loan

Background: The conventional loan is the plain Jane of home loans. It's not a government-backed loan, but meets the requirements set by Fannie Mae and Freddie Mac, which are two government-sponsored agencies. Lenders have a wide variety of conventional loan products. Some even allow for a low down payment. Shopping around is the key to getting the best conventional loan.

Eligibility requirements:

- **Down payment:** As low as 3%, but can be higher for conventional loans
- **Credit score:** 620; 640 to 720 or higher preferred
- **Debt-to-income ratio (DTI):** Up to 50%

Other conventional loan details:

- **Sellers assist may be allowed:** Sellers can contribute anywhere from 2% to 9% of the sales price to your costs depending on your down payment. Most lenders want you to have the funds for your own down payment and will allow you to use seller concessions towards closing and other settlement costs.
    - **General rules:**
    - **Down payment under 10%:** Seller concession up to 3%
    - **Down payment between 10-25%:** Seller concession up to 6%
    - **Down payment 25% or more:** Seller concession up to 9%

- **Wait period after adverse credit history:**
    - **Discharged Chapter 7 bankruptcy:** Four-year wait.
    - **Discharged Chapter 13 bankruptcy:** Two-year wait.
    - **Deed in lieu or short sale:** Four-year wait.
    - **Foreclosure:** Seven-year wait.

Your Task

After reading through these popular home loans, your task is to pick out the home loan you are considering.

You can do a bit of independent research on the loans to get more details. Keep in mind that the above is just an overview. There's quite a bit of nuance to home loans and different lenders can have different requirements.

After you're finished with that task, you're done for the day!

Home loans I'm considering...

Live Richer Challenge: Homebuying Edition
Day 11: Ways to Save

Today's Easy Financial Task: Developing a savings strategy.

How to rock this task:
- Decide how much you want to save for your new home.
- Pull out your budget and bills to find savings opportunities.
- Set up a savings account for your home fund.

Welcome to Day 11 of the LRC: Homebuying Challenge!

The first few days of this week we talked about your credit and capital. We also discussed popular home loans and what they require as far as credit, DTI and down payment. Today is all about developing a savings strategy for your next home.

Based on the loans discussed yesterday, you should have an idea of what you're going to need for a down payment. It's time to start saving!

How to Focus on Saving
When preparing for a home, budgeting and saving need to become a priority months or years in advance. (If you don't have a budget, I can teach you how to make one quickly in my book, *The One Week Budget*. Grab a chapter for free on www.livericherchallenge.com, Day 11).

The place to start when saving for a home is writing down a savings goal you want to reach by a certain time. Then, calculate how much you need to save monthly to meet your goal. Say you want to save an extra $4,000 for a down payment and closing costs. You need to save just $334 per month for a year.

Where could this money come from? I'm glad you asked. :)

Cut excess spending from your budget
An area of opportunity is often variable expenses. Variable expenses are the ones that can fluctuate from month to month like gas, groceries, eating out, installing a lace front, and more.

Take a close look at your monthly budget and find places where you can make cuts. Don't worry — you don't have to give up this stuff forever, only until you're able to get the keys to your new home!

Negotiate your fixed expenses
Fixed expenses can be reduced too! Here are the steps:

1. **Pull out the bills for each provider.** Look at your bills and review the prices you pay for services like telephone, internet, cable, insurance, and more.
2. **Comparison shop.** Start looking around for competitors to compare prices.
3. **Negotiate with your current provider.** If you find a better rate, call your currentprovider with the price you found. Tell them you're going to bounce to the newprovider if it can't be matched.
4. **Ask to speak to the retention department.** This is the last ditch effort. It's the retention department's job to retain customers. Explain the new rates you've found and let them know you'll be leaving if they can't match them. If they can match the rate — yay! If they can't, move on to step five.
5. **Jump ship to the new provider.** Switch providers to the cheaper one, if necessary.

Refinance your present debt
Refinancing your current debt is another way to find savings. Refinancing debt can lower your interest rate. It can even make your interest rate 0%. Refinancing is when you pay off your current debt with another, more affordable debt vehicle.

Here are two popular options:
- **Personal loans:** Personal loans with a low and fixed interest rate could be used to pay off your credit card and other high-interest debt. Personal loans give you one convenient, stable payment to keep up with each month.

- **Balance transfer cards:** Balance transfer cards are awesome, and offer an introductory rate for new customers. The rate can be as low as 0% for 15 months or more. This gives you an opportunity to pay your balances back interest-free. The savings can be put towards your homebuying fund!

Note: If you plan to consolidate or refinance your debt, make sure you do this 6 months BEFORE you start shopping for a home. These options will require credit checks and can disrupt the mortgage process.

Where should you be putting your money?
After you think of areas in your budget where you can save, the last task for today is to set up a separate account for your home savings. The best accounts for savings are ones that aren't easily accessible. Don't create an account that's connected to your checking account that you can spend! **Instead, open a new account!**

I love online accounts for savings. These accounts have no fees. It also takes a long time for money to transfer from savings to your checking with an online bank, which can deter you from overspending!

My favorite online account is the savings account by Ally Bank. Find out how to sign up for one on www.livericherchallenge.com book resources page, Day 11! This bank has no annual fees, and no minimum balance is required to open.

Once your savings account is set up, you can create an automatic deposit from your checking to your savings. The automatic payment should be the amount of money you need to save each month to meet your homebuying money goal.

You can break this savings deposit into two withdrawals from checking that will happen twice per month if that's easier to manage. The best way to save is to take the flawed human (you) out of the equation.

When savings is automated, it can grow with minimal effort from you!

That's all for this task! See you in the next one!

Live Richer Challenge: Homebuying Edition
Day 12: Special Housing Programs

Today's Easy Financial Task: Learn about special homebuying programs.

How to rock this task:
- Read the guidelines for a few low-cost homebuying programs.
- Write down any homebuying programs you're considering for your next purchase.
- Start researching state-specific housing programs that are available in your area.

Woot woot! We're at the final day of this week. Give yourself a round of applause! Today we're going to dig into some low-cost homebuying programs that are available.

Special housing and down payment assistance programs are typically for low-to-moderate income households that need assistance buying a home. These programs make the dream of homeownership possible for homebuyers who may have trouble buying a home without a helping hand.

You have two tasks today:

1. Familiarize yourself with the homebuying programs listed below.
2. Research other state and local programs near you.

In this task, we'll be discussing NACA, Habitat for Humanity, Good Neighbor Next Door, and HUD Dollar Homes. Let's get started!

NACA
You've probably heard of NACA before, and are wondering what it's all about. NACA, or The Neighborhood Assistance Corporation of America, is a non-profit that gives eligible homebuyers the chance to purchase their home with no down payment and no closing costs. The lender takes care of the appraisal fees, transfer taxes, title insurance, and all that good stuff.

Perfect credit isn't necessary. The program is for low-to-moderate income households and those who are buying in low-to-moderate income communities.

The real beauty of this program is that it offers highly competitive interest rates on 15-year and 30-year mortgages despite the lenient eligibility criteria. There's also no mortgage insurance required, even with no down payment! (We'll talk about what mortgage insurance is next week!)

The program can be used for single-family homes, condos, multi-family homes, co-ops, rehabs, and mixed-use property.

Here's a summary of how the NACA process works:
- Attend a NACA homebuyer workshop. Learn more at naca.com.
- Schedule a meeting with a counselor.
- Choose an agent and notify NACA.
- Start searching for a home.
- Fill out NACA home qualification and mortgage paperwork when you're ready to buy.
- Close on the home.

This is just an overview of the process. The first two steps — attending a NACA workshop and meeting with a counselor, will give you a better understanding of what to expect from start to finish.

Habitat for Humanity
Habitat for Humanity may be another affordable option to consider, as long as you're willing to get your hands a bit dirty for a good cause. Homebuyers build their home and receive an affordable mortgage through the Habitat for Humanity program. The money received from these mortgages goes back into building more houses.

To be eligible for Habitat for Humanity, you must:
- Show a need for safe and affordable housing.

- Be willing to build a home and help build other people's homes that are part of the program.
- Be able to afford mortgage payments.

Learn more about applying at www.habitat.org.

Good Neighbor Next Door
Good Neighbor Next Door is a unique program for law enforcement officers, teachers, firefighters, and EMTs. The HUD's Good Neighbor Next Door program offers a deal of 50% off the list price of an eligible home for these professionals. There are stipulations and qualifications for the program. The home has to be in a revitalization area and be listed through the program. You also have to live in the home for at least three years.

HUD Dollar Homes
The HUD Dollar Homes program is also available if you earn low-to-moderate income, and you're willing to live in a neighborhood that needs revitalization. These homes are purchased for $1 each. The purpose of the program is to encourage restoration and occupation of homes in designated neighborhoods that are in need of development.

Local and State Programs
Lastly, there are local and state programs that you should research. Down payment assistance programs can be offered by state or local housing authorities and non-profits. Some programs are geared toward first-time homebuyers, while others allow repeat buyers to participate.

Here are some places to look during your search:

- **State Housing Finance Agencies:** These organizations are vital to your search and are not difficult to find. Every state has a housing finance agency (HFA). You can Google your state and the words "housing finance agency" and yours should pop up. This is a phenomenal place to start, as your local office can provide free counseling and housing educational courses specific to down payment assistance programs.

- **City/County Specific Programs:** Researching your city's offerings is also a great place to start, especially if you live in a big city. Again, Google is your friend. Search "housing programs" and your state, city, and county.
- **Private Non-Profit Organizations:** There are some really good charitable organizations that help people buy their first home. These groups often work with or through your state and local government housing agencies and their approved lenders. You may be able to find these programs on your state's housing agency website.

Your Tasks

After reading an overview of the programs above, your last task for today is to do a bit of research on these programs. Choose a few you may want to consider and search for state and local programs that may benefit you in the homebuying process. Sharing is caring. Share with your accountability partner(s).

We've reached the end of the second week of tasks!

You're two-thirds of the way through the LRC: Homebuying Edition! Woot woot!

At this point, you should feel more confident in your knowledge of what's required to buy a home.

The homebuying programs I'm considering...

_____

_____

_____

_____

_____

_____

Live Richer Challenge: Homebuying Edition
Day 13: Review, Reflect, Relax

Today's Easy Financial Task: Review, Reflect, Relax

How to rock this task:
- *Review* this week's LRC: Homebuying Edition tasks.
- *Reflect* on what we've learned this week.
- *Relax.* In two days we start Week 3: The Home Loan Process.

Welcome to Day 13 of the challenge! Hey hey, we've made it to the end of the second week of the Live Richer Challenge! Take this day to review, reflect, and relax.

Today is also a great day to check in on your accountability partner(s). Do they need help with a task? Do they need some encouragement? Do you both need to catch up on past tasks? Go back through this week.

Live Richer Challenge: Homebuying Edition
Day 14: Weekly Inspiration

Week 2: Home Loan Requirements

Today's Easy Financial Task: Watch the Week 2 Dream Catcher Hangout chat.

How to rock this task:
- Watch the video.
- Listen to words of encouragement.
- Complete challenge tasks you missed.

Today's our second Dream Catcher Hangout chat! During the video, we'll discuss the tasks we've worked on this week. We'll also talk about the key takeaways and you'll hear how other Dream Catchers are working through the challenge. Make sure to check in on your accountability partner. Have they completed the first and second weeks?

FYI: After watching the video, today is also a good day to catch up on any tasks that you missed throughout the week.

Watch the Dream Catcher Hangout at www.livericherchallenge.com, Week 2, Day 14: Weekly Inspiration.

The Home Loan Process Recap Checklist
Week 2

This Week's Goal: To understand how credit plays a role in the homebuying process and learn the eligibility requirements for popular homebuying programs.

- **Day 8:** Your Character
  - **Easy Financial Task:** Get your credit reports and scores.

- **Day 9:** Your Capital
  - **Easy Financial Task:** Determine how much money you have for a home purchase.

- **Day 10:** Popular Home Loans
  - **Easy Financial Task:** Learn about various home loan products.

- **Day 11:** Ways to Save
  - **Easy Financial Task:** Develop a savings strategy.

- **Day 12:** Special Housing Programs
  - **Easy Financial Task:** Learn about special homebuying programs.

- **Day 13:** Review, Reflect, Relax
  - **Easy Financial Task:** Review, Reflect, Relax.

- **Day 14:** Weekly Inspiration
  - **Easy Financial Task:** Watch the Week 2 Dream Catcher Hangout chat.

Week 2 Reflections

WEEK 3: THE HOME LOAN PROCESS

THIS WEEK'S GOAL:

To learn the people who help you buy a home and how the homebuying process works.

Live Richer Challenge: Homebuying Edition
Day 15: Your Collateral

Today's Easy Financial Task: Learn what collateral is and how it impacts your home purchase.

How to rock this task:
- Watch the video.
- Understand how collateral plays a role in homebuying.
- Learn how lenders determine the value of a home through an appraisal.

Welcome to the last week of the LRC: Homebuying Edition!

Give yourself a hand clap for making it this far in the challenge! This week we have a new set of tasks to help you on your journey to becoming a homeowner. So far, we've tackled four of the 5 C's of Credit, including capacity, character and capital.

Today we're going to talk about **collateral.**

Before we get started, today's our last video day! Watch the video for today at www.livericherchallenge.com, Day 15.

What's collateral?
Collateral is an asset that secures a loan. When buying a home, your property is what secures the home loan. If you don't keep up with the payments, your lender can take the home (aka the collateral) and sell it to pay off your loan.

Why Lenders Need to Determine the Value of Your Home
You've probably heard of the term appraisal before.

An appraisal is done by a lender to determine how much the home you're buying is worth. Lenders do an appraisal to make sure they are lending you an appropriate amount of money for the home you're buying. **Why?** If they take the home, they want it to be worth what you borrowed.

What happens during an appraisal?
The appraiser will estimate the market value of the home. It is typically ordered by the lender and should be done by an unbiased party to ensure they give an unbiased estimate. The appraiser will look at:

- Location
- Size of the home
- Age of the home
- How many rooms in the home
- How much other homes in the market have sold for

The result of the appraisal is the appraisal report. It typically takes a few days for the appraisal report to come back. At that time, you (the buyer) or the seller can raise questions about the findings.

How does the appraisal impact the buyer?
The seller is on the hot seat during the appraisal. They're hoping the home comes back at a value that's acceptable to the lender.

However, the appraisal is an important aspect of the deal for you to pay attention to as well. Purchasing a home can be an emotional decision, but it's also a *business* one.

Selecting the right location and property is important for you AND the lender. You want to choose a home in an area where the value of your home can soar. This will be important when you sell the home.

After you watch the video and read through what an appraisal is, that's the end of today's task. See you in the next one! Make sure to check in with your accountability partner(s).

Live Richer Challenge: Homebuying Edition
Day 16: Mortgage Insurance

Today's Easy Financial Task: Learn what mortgage insurance is and how it relates to your mortgage.

How to rock this task:
- Learn the situations where you may have to pay mortgage insurance.
- Look for mortgage products where lenders pay mortgage insurance.

Welcome to the 16th day of the LRC: Homebuying Edition!

Today we're going to talk about mortgage insurance! If you have no idea what mortgage insurance is, don't worry. You'll know how it works by the end of this task!

What is mortgage insurance?
Mortgage insurance is something a lender may charge when you put less than 20% down on a home. The purpose of mortgage insurance is to protect the lender if you stop paying since you put less money into the home upfront. Mortgage insurance can range from 0.30 to 1.5% of the original loan amount per year.

Some low down payment mortgages require insurance, while others don't.

For example, NACA is a low down payment program we discussed last week that doesn't require mortgage insurance.

How do you pay mortgage insurance?
You usually make payments towards your motgage insurance each month as part of your mortgage payment.

There are also situations where the lender will pay the mortgage insurance. This is ideal! When a lender pays the insurance, it's called lender-paid mortgage insurance.

Navy Federal Credit Union is an example of a lender that will pay the mortgage insurance on your behalf.

Mortgage Insurance for Different Loan Programs
Different loan programs call mortgage insurance a different name, but for the most part, the insurance works the same in each scenario.

Here's a breakdown of the mortgage insurance rules for popular loans:

The FHA loan
The FHA loan (the loan backed by the Federal Housing Administration requiring as low as 3.5% down) has what's called mortgage insurance premiums (MIP).

You pay upfront mortgage insurance premiums and an annual premium that's broken down into monthly payments. The upfront premiums may be rolled into your mortgage so you don't have to pay the upfront fees out-of-pocket.

The VA loan
The VA loan for veterans does not have "mortgage insurance" technically, but there is a funding fee that's similar to insurance and is a percentage of the home loan amount. The funding fee is an upfront fee, but you can roll it into your mortgage to pay monthly as well.

The USDA loan
The USDA loan (for people who live in rural and suburban areas) has an upfront guarantee fee and an annual fee that is like insurance. The upfront guarantee fee may also be added to your mortgage so you don't have to pay it at closing. The annual fee is split into installment payments that you pay monthly.

Conventional loan

The insurance that you pay for a conventional loan is called private mortgage insurance (PMI). Private mortgage insurance is one where lenders may pay the mortgage insurance for you. **The best thing to do is shop around with multiple lenders to see what they can offer.**

When does mortgage insurance go away?

The number of years you have to pay mortgage insurance depends on the loan program. In some cases, when the equity you have in the home gets to 20% (this means you've paid off your loan enough to where it's like you put 20% down on the home), you can ask to have the mortgage insurance removed.

In other instances, you can refinance the mortgage to remove insurance. A refinance is when you get a new loan that doesn't have insurance to pay off your old loan. **Speak with your mortgage provider to understand what the rules are for your mortgage program.**

Your Task

Your task today is to look for lenders that pay mortgage insurance.

Government-backed loan programs like the FHA, VA, USDA, and conventional loans may have lender-paid insurance — you have to look around.

Not sure where to look? Try local credit unions and other local financial institutions, then write down what you find.

Lenders that offer lender-paid insurance...

_____

_____

_____

_____

Live Richer Challenge: Homebuying Edition
Day 17: Compliance

Today's Easy Financial Task: Start researching the housing market where you want to buy.

How to rock this task:
- Learn the compliance factor of the 5 C's of Credit.
- Do market research in the location where you intend to buy.

Another day, another task!

In this task, we're talking about the last "C" of the 5 C's of Credit. Get excited! We've gone through capacity, character, capital, and collateral. The last "C" is compliance, which is sometimes called conditions.

The Compliance Factor
Compliance has to do with the 'big picture.'

Compliance is a look beyond your personal financial situation. Lenders check out what's going on in the housing market to determine whether they want to lend to you and at what cost.

The lender will consider:
Inventory: Inventory is the number of homes for sale. A buyer's market is when there is a lot of inventory. Buyers have a bit more leeway when negotiating on costs in a buyer's market because there are more people selling homes than buying. Lenders may be willing to do what's necessary to close deals when fewer buyers apply for mortgages. This is a good time to buy a house. You have leverage! In a seller's market, there are more buyers than there are homes. Competition for homes is tight, and lenders may be less willing to negotiate because there's a higher demand for homes and mortgages. The inventory and what the housing market is doing will impact the terms lenders are willing to offer.

Interest rates: Lenders will also take a look at the market to determine what your interest rate will be. Lenders don't set random numbers for interest rates; there are indexes and other factors that go into setting rates besides your credit.

The local housing market: Lenders look at the local housing market to see what homes are selling for and how the home you are buying compares.

The overall economy: Lenders look at what's happening with the local economy and how it could impact your financial situation. For example, if the biggest employer in your area is closing up shop, it may impact how much money they are willing to lend to homebuyers.

Your Task
Moving on to your task! Your task today is to start doing some research on the housing market in the area where you want to buy.

Here are some questions to think about:
• What's the pricing in my area?
• Where are interest rates right now?
• What is the inventory looking like?
• Are there a lot of homes available right now or not so much?

You can consult with a realtor to answer these questions. A professional can give you greater insight into how the market is for your locale.

For this task, start looking consistently at Zillow.com, Realtor.com, or Trulia. Get familiar with the pricing for your area and how long the homes are staying on the market.

If homes are moving slowly, that can be good news for you! Sellers having trouble selling their homes may be willing to offer a deal. That's it for this task!

Write down any information you find about pricing, interest rates, and inventory...

Live Richer Challenge: Homebuying Edition
Day 18: Your Home Team

Today's Easy Financial Task: Learn what mortgage insurance is and how it relates to your mortgage.

How to rock this task:
- Come up with two to three professionals that offer the services you need and interview them.

Welcome to Day 18 of the LRC: Homebuying Challenge!

Today is the second to last day of the week. How have you been enjoying this week so far? How is your accountability partner(s) doing? Make sure you check in with them regularly. Teamwork makes the dream work!

In this task, we're going to talk about your home team. These are the important players in your home purchase.

You don't do all of this alone. Instead, you assemble an awesome crew to help you navigate the homebuying process.

Your task is to read through the different people who should be on your homebuying team and what they do.

Next, start researching professionals within the respective fields and choose two to three individuals. **When you begin actively searching for a home, call up these people for your home team and interview them.** Ask about their credentials, get an idea of how responsive they are, and determine if you're confident in their abilities.

When buying a home, you need to think of yourself as the client.

All of the people on your home team are working for you, which is why you want to interview them before working together. Make sure they're reliable and a good fit. Working with people you trust makes the home-buying process muuuch better!

Here are the people who will help you when buying a home:

Your Agent
Your agent assists you in searching for and buying a home. They'll help you put in an offer and negotiate the deal.

The Lender
A lender is the one who lends the money you need to purchase the home. The lender is typically a bank, credit union, or mortgage company. The person you closely work with is usually called the loan officer. They are the ones who collect your paperwork, ask you questions, and give you instructions throughout the process.

The Appraiser
We talked about appraisals earlier this week. The lender chooses this person, but it's worthwhile to mention it here. The appraiser is the person who decides what the property is worth.

The Title Company
The title company does a title search and issues title insurance. A title search is when a search is done to make sure no one else has a claim on the property. For example, the government could have a claim on it for unpaid taxes. Title insurance is an insurance policy offered to the buyer and the lender after the title search is done. This insurance protects you in case someone comes out of the woodwork and says that the home belongs to them after you buy.

Home Inspector
The home inspector is the person who inspects the home to see if there are any problems with it before you buy. The home inspection is an important part of the process and you need to hire someone good. This is the person who is going to make sure you're not making a bad investment! I'm grateful for hiring a quality home inspector when I was going

to buy an investment property. I found out the home had far more problems than it was worth before buying. Thankfully, I could back out of the deal! The American Society of Home Inspectors may be a good place to start your search on licensed inspectors.

Home Insurance Provider
Homeowners need home insurance. Generally, lenders want to see that you have home insurance before settling your home loan. It's a good idea to start comparing home insurance rates. Getting insurance quotes from multiple providers will help you find one that can offer you the very best deal.

On to Your Task
For today's task, come up with two to three individuals for your home team. Not sure where to look? Referrals are the BEST place to find awesome people to add to your

Use this section to write down recommendations and people you research to add to your home team…

_____

_____

_____

_____

_____

_____

_____

_____

_____

Live Richer Challenge: Homebuying Edition
Day 19: The Loan Process

Today's Easy Financial Task: Learn the steps of the homebuying process and collect all the documents you need.

How to rock this task:
- Read through the stages of homebuying.
- Create a digital folder to store the documents you need.

Welcome to the last day of this week! After today, you'll have two days to review what we've covered thus far. Today I'm going to give you an overview of the homebuying process!

The Home Loan Process
Here are the steps to buying a home:

- **Get your documents together.** Putting your financial documents together beforehand helps speed up the application process. (We'll talk about the documents you need below). Lenders and agents prefer to work with borrowers who have their stuff together.

- **Shop around for a mortgage and get pre-approved.** Very often, people go right into the home search, but getting pre-approved for a mortgage first has its benefits. A pre-approval is when a lender conditionally approves you for a home loan. They check your credit, income, and other documents to give you a conditional amount that they're willing to give you in a pre-approval letter. You can take this letter with you when looking for an agent and to show sellers. A pre-approval shows that you're serious about buying.

- **Choose an agent and start looking for homes.** An agent will help you look for homes. They can also give you advice about the housing market and may have the inside scoop on home listings.

- **Put in an offer.** When you find a home, the agent will help you put in an offer.

- **Respond to any counteroffers.** Homebuying can include negotiations! The seller of the home may come back with a counteroffer. You and your agent can decide whether to accept the offer or issue another counteroffer. This is when some back and forth can happen! Don't get discouraged!

- **Do a home inspection.** Your home inspector will do a review of the home to see if there are any defects like an old roof or insect damage. Typically, an offer is contingent on a home inspection. This means that you're making an offer with the understanding that you can back out of the deal if the home inspection isn't up to par.

- **Home Appraisal.** The lender does the appraisal to determine the value of the home.

- **Your lender will process the loan.** Your loan pre-approval is not a final approval. The loan will go through underwriting to give you a final response. If all goes well, you'll get a closing date!

- **Final walk through.** The final walkthrough is the last chance for you to make any final requests about the home.

- **Home loan closing.** Today is the big day! Closing is when the money (down payment and any other required funds) exchanges hands. You sign final documents and get the keys to your home!

The Documents You Need

The task today is to assemble the documents you need to give to your lender to get pre-approved. Gather these documents:

- W-2s and paystubs
- 1099s
- Other proof of income
  (aka pension income, social security, child support, alimony)
- Tax returns for two years
- Rental history
- Bank statements for a two-month period
- Debt account statements
- Investment accounts
- Profit and loss statement if self-employed

The great thing about starting your digital folder is that you can always keep it updated. Not ready to buy a house within the next few months or even a year? No problem. Just keep adding to your folder. When you are ready to buy, you'll have the stuff you need organized.

We've reached the end of week 3!

At this point, you should feel more confident in your knowledge of what's required to buy a home. You should also know the steps of homebuying and people who help you along the way.

Live Richer Challenge: Homebuying Edition
Day 20: Review, Reflect, Relax

Today's Easy Financial Task: Review, Reflect, Relax

How to rock this task:
- *Review* this week's Live Richer Challenge: Homebuying Edition tasks.
- *Reflect* on what we've learned this week.
- *Relax*. The last day of the challenge is in two days!

You've completed the third week of the Live Richer Challenge: Homebuying Edition! Woot, woot! Take this day to review, reflect, and relax.

Today is also a great day to check in on your accountability partner(s). Do they need help with a task? Do they need some encouragement? Do you both need to catch up on past tasks? Go back through this week.

Lastly, as you continue to work towards finishing out your homebuying goals, here's some questions to ask yourself:

- How strong is your financial foundation?
- Is it in alignment with your homeownership goals?
- If not, what's holding you back and what steps are you taking to strengthen it?

If you're not sure where to start, head to livericherchallenge.com and sign-up for the Savings Edition. It's a perfect compliment to this Challenge.

Live Richer Challenge: Homebuying Edition
Day 21: Weekly Inspiration

Today's Easy Financial Task: Watch the Week 3 Dream Catcher Hangout chat.

How to rock this task:
- Watch the video.
- Listen to words of encouragement.
- Complete challenge tasks you missed.

Today's our third and last Dream Catcher Hangout chat of the LRC: Homebuying Edition! During the video, we'll discuss the tasks we've worked on this week. We'll also talk about key takeaways, and you'll hear how other Dream Catchers are working through the challenge.

FYI: Today is a good day to catch up on any tasks that you missed throughout the week. Watch the Dream Catcher Hangout at www.livericherchallenge.com, Week 3, Day 21: Weekly Inspiration.

> Did you know that you're one day away from finishing this Challenge? Yay! Let's celebrate! Head to ShopLiveRicher.com and rock your new, official Dream Catcher status with a t-shirt that shows the world who you are!

DAY 22: LIVE RICHER

FINAL DAY'S GOAL:

To visualize the home you want and start the process of turning your dream home into a reality.

Live Richer Challenge: Homebuying Edition
Day 22: LIVE RICHER

Today's Easy Financial Task: Celebrate completing the challenge and do the "Dream Home" activity.

How to rock this task:
- Give yourself a hand clap for finishing the LRC: Homebuying Edition.
- Do the "Dream Home" activity.

Cue a round of applause!

You've made it to the final day of the LRC: Homebuying Edition! For the last three weeks, we've covered what you need to qualify for a home and how the homebuying process works.

Did you have a good time? I know I did!

I have one last fun activity for you today to wrap up the challenge. It's called the "Dream Home" activity. Today, you're going to start visualizing the home you want and doing some research to get your search started.

Now that you have an idea of how much home you can afford and the different mortgage products that are available, let's bring your dream home into focus.

This activity is one that will probably take you a few days.
For today's task, you should at least do steps 1-6.

Here's what you need to do:

Step 1: Write down three of your desired neighborhoods.
The first step in this activity is to pull out a piece of paper and write down three neighborhoods you're thinking about living in.

Step 2: Write down your monthly home payment budget.
Next step! After working through this challenge, you should have an idea of how much home you can afford and the monthly payment you can manage.

Keep in mind, you may not want to buy a home at the very top of your budget. For example, say your lender is willing to give you a home loan with a $2,000 home payment per month. Technically speaking, you can afford this amount because the lender is willing to give you the money, but it may be not the right choice for your budget.

Spending too much on your home payment can result in you becoming what's called "house poor." House poor is when you have a fabulous home, but you hardly have enough money left over to furnish or maintain it. NOT GOOD! You do not want to be house poor. With all of this in mind, write down how much you would be comfortable paying each month on a mortgage given your current salary and expenses.

Step 3: Write the amount you want to put down.
On Day 10 of the challenge, we went through various home loans including the FHA, VA, USDA, and a conventional loan. For this step, write down the loan programs you're considering and the down payment required.

For example, if you want to go the FHA route, there's the 3.5% to 10% down payment. For conventional loans, you may be required to put closer to 20% down. If you need a refresher on the loans and what they require, go back to Day 10.

Step 4: Write down the current home loan interest.
Interest rates are the next thing you want to write down. Market interest rates can change from week to week. Lenders determine your rate after taking a look at your credit. For this step, get a general sense of what interest rates are doing right now. Head over to BankRate.com to review current rates. You're most likely looking at the 30-year fixed rate mortgage option. This means the loan term spans 30 years and the rate is fixed over the entire loan term.

Step 5: Start looking for homes and write down a few prices.

Last week, you did some research to see what's going on in the overall housing market. For the "Dream Home" activity, I want you to start looking specifically at the homes you love in your desired neighborhoods. How much do they cost? You can check Zillow.com, Realtor.com, and Trulia.com for pricing. If the homes are outside of your price range, start looking at areas adjacent to these neighborhoods. Write down the prices of homes that you like.

Step 6: Use the calculator to play with the numbers.

Take the numbers you have (the down payment you have available, the interest rate, and home prices) and type them into a mortgage calendar. Play with the numbers to see how the monthly payment changes. Look to see what happens to the payment when you put more money down. Look to see what happens to the payment when you put in a lower home price.

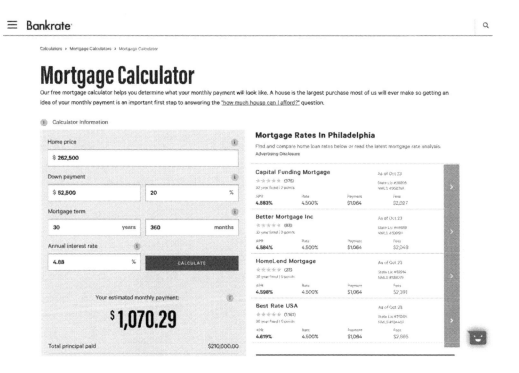

Step 7: Take a trip.
Hop in the car and take a trip to the neighborhoods you're interested in. Take pictures of houses, businesses, and other locations in the area to see if it's a good fit. For instance, check out the schools and how far they are to your home. You can also head over to Google Maps to see if there are shopping malls around or other stores and restaurants nearby. This step is to help you get a lay of the land.

Step 8: Continue to build your portfolio.
Last step! This "Dream Home" activity is the start of your home wish list. Keep all of this information above and build a portfolio of pictures of homes and areas you like. You can create a folder for the portfolio on your laptop or tablet. Cut out pictures from magazines of homes, decor, and furniture so you can visualize your new home.

Finish this task and you've completed the entire LRC: Homebuying Edition!

The fun doesn't stop here though! We have many more courses and live sessions from experts if you join our Live Richer Academy at www.livericheracademy.com

It's a school where I provide resources to continue your journey to becoming wealthy and financially free. The Live Richer online community is also a place that's poppin' all year round with experts and other Dream Builders who are serious about building wealth.

Thank you for participating. You're a rockstar and truly a Dream Catcher!

The Home Loan Process Recap Checklist
Week 3

This Week's Goal: To learn how the homebuying process works.

- **Day 15:** Your Collateral
  - ○ **Easy Financial Task:** Learn what collateral is and how it impacts yourhome purchase.

- **Day 16:** Mortgage Insurance
  - ○ **Easy Financial Task:** Learn what mortgage insurance is and how it relates to your mortgage.

- **Day 17:** Compliance
  - ○ **Easy Financial Task:** Start researching the housing market where you want to buy.

- **Day 18:** Your Home Team
  - ○ **Easy Financial Task:** Learn about the people who help you buy a home.

- **Day 19:** The Loan Process
  - ○ **Easy Financial Task:** Learn the steps of the homebuying process and collect all the documents you need.

- **Day 20:** Review, Reflect, Relax
  - ○ **Easy Financial Task:** Review, Reflect, Relax.

- **Day 21:** Weekly Inspiration
  - ○ **Easy Financial Task:** Watch the Week 3 Dream Catcher Hangout chat.

- **Day 22:** Live Richer
  - ○ **Easy Financial Task:** Celebrate completing the Challenge and complete the "Dream Home" activity.

LIVE RICHER Challenge Reflections

Acknowledgments:

First and foremost, I would like to give my most grateful thanks to God. He always blesses us. It is we who allow or do not allow our blessings to manifest.

I also want to thank Mommy, Daddy, and my sisters: Karen, Tracy, Carol, and Lisa. You are my cheerleaders, my best friends, my sounding board, and my inspiration. Anyone who knows the Aliche girls knows how supportive we are of each other. Thank you.

To all my family, both here and abroad, thank you for your constant love and support. The strong foundation you've provided is the reason I've been able to reach such heights.

Taylor Medine and Tanya Williams, thank you so much for helping me transform and polish my words into a book I can be proud of.

Superman, Jerrell, my husband, thank you for your unwavering support and love.

Thank you to my designer Hector Torres with the typesetting assitance of Stefanie Tam. I came to you at crunch time and you more than delivered.

Thank you, Karen Maine and Logan Gamble. I literally could not have launched this LIVE RICHER Challenge without you.

Jubril Agoro, thank you for helping me to amplify my voice.

Special thanks to all my family, friends, coworkers, and all of my well-wishers.

To the rest of the Unicorn squad, you make MAGIC happen each and every day. Thank for all that you do and give. You're more than a team, you are my sisters and brothers. :)

Lastly, I especially want to thank you. Yes, you reading these words. You allowed me to help you LIVE RICHER. You gave me more than I ever gave you. I am forever grateful.

Live richer,
Tiffany

Tiffany "The Budgetnista" Aliche is a highly sought-after expert and voice in the big, sometimes scary, world of finance. - Black Enterprise

An Amazon #1 bestselling author (The One Week Budget and Live Richer Challenge), a sought-after speaker and teacher of financial empowerment, Tiffany is quickly becoming America's favorite, personal financial educator. The Budgetnista's movement has inspired and empowered hundreds of thousands of women worldwide to achieve their financial goals.

Since 2008, The Budgetnista has served as brand ambassador and spokesperson for countless corporate and non-profit organizations – delivering her engaging financial education through seminars, workshops, curriculum and training.

In 2014, Tiffany founded the LIVE RICHER Challenge Movement; a powerful virtual community of over 700,000 thousand women from 100+ countries. In 2017, The Budgetnista landed a guest spot on the Emmy-nominated talk show, The Real, as their go-to personal finance expert.

Her financial advice has also been featured in The New York Times, Reuters, US News and World Report, the TODAY show, Good Morning America, CNN, PBS, Fox Business, MSNBC, CBS MoneyWatch, TIME, ESSENCE Magazine, Entrepreneur Magazine, Black Enterprise, and FORBES.

Tiffany has been a featured speaker at American Express, Princeton University, JetBlue, Wyndham Worldwide, Columbia University, Circle of Sisters, MegaFest, The United Way, Prudential Financial Inc. and more. She also blogs about personal finance for The Huffington Post and co-hosts an award-winning podcast, Brown Ambition.

Learn more about Tiffany and The Budgetnista here: thebudgetnista.com.

Made in United States
Troutdale, OR
09/17/2023